MARY
KAY
Cosmetics Queen

Laurie Rozakis

ROURKE ENTERPRISES,INC.
VERO BEACH, FLORIDA 32964

A Blackbirch Graphics book.

Library of Congress Cataloging-in-Publication Data

Rozakis, Laurie.
   Mary Kay / by Laurie Rozakis.
     p.   cm. — (Made in America)
   Includes bibliographical references and index.
   Summary: A biography of the woman who developed her business philosophy by creating her own cosmetics company.
   ISBN 0-86592-040-0
   1. Ash, Mary Kay—Juvenile literature. 2. Women in business—United States—Biography—Juvenile literature.
3. Mary Kay Cosmetics—History—Juvenile literature. [1. Ash, Mary Kay. 2. Businesswomen. 3. Mary Kay Cosmetics—History.] I. Series.
HD9970.5.C672A836 1993
3812'.456685'092—dc20
[B]   92-45124
                                               CIP
                                               AC

Contents

1

"You Can Do It, Mary Kay!"

"Even though some of my duties were supposed to be too difficult for a child, nobody ever told me that....I just did them."

It was still dark at five o'clock in the morning when Mrs. Wagner went to work. Softly, she kissed her seven-year-old daughter, Mary Kathlyn, goodbye. Fourteen hours later, when she returned home, her daughter was already asleep.

When Mary Kathlyn Wagner was a small child, her father became very ill. He had a lung disease called tuberculosis. In the 1920s, there was still no cure. People were sent to special hospitals known as sanatoriums. They were given good food

Opposite: Mary Kay brought a unique approach to selling cosmetics and became one of America's most successful businesspeople.

and a lot of rest. Mr. Wagner was still very sick when he came home. Since he could not work, Mary Kay's mother had to support the family. Mrs. Wagner was a nurse, but she could not make enough money to support her family by nursing. She became a restaurant manager. The job did not pay well, and because she was a woman Mrs. Wagner got even less money than men who were restaurant managers. Mary Kay's older brother and sister had already grown up and left the house. Young Mary Kay had to take care of her father, the house, and herself all at the same time.

Keeping House

Every afternoon, little Mary Kay came home from school and cleaned the house. When everything was spick-and-span, she sat down to do her homework. Then came her biggest challenge: cooking. There were no prepared meals, large freezers, fast food, or microwave ovens in the 1920s. Every meal had to be made fresh, on the spot. Mary Kay's mother could not be home to teach her daughter how to cook. Her father was too ill to get out of bed. What did Mary Kay do? She called her mother at the restaurant for lessons. Every night, Mrs.

As a young girl, Mary Kay was left to care for her sick father while her mother worked to support her family.

Wagner would carefully explain the steps in the recipe.

"Hi, Mother," said Mary Kay, "Daddy wants potato soup for dinner tonight. How do I make it?"

"Okay, honey. First you get out the big pot, the one you used yesterday. Then you take out two potatoes. . . ."

Step by step, Mrs. Wagner explained to her daughter how to prepare the meal. At the end of the phone call, she always said, "Honey, *you can do it.*"

Shopping on Her Own

Besides cleaning and cooking, Mary Kay also had to buy all her own clothing. In the 1920s, Houston, Texas, had streetcars to take people to the shopping area. Streetcars were small vehicles that traveled down tracks in the street. Most Saturdays, Mary Kay took a streetcar by herself to the stores in downtown Houston. Her mother was working, and her friends were not allowed to go on the streetcars without a parent. Mrs. Wagner would carefully explain to Mary Kay how to take the streetcar, buy her clothing and lunch, and return home. "Honey, *I know you can do it*," she said. Then she would give her daughter $1.50, which was a lot of money in the 1920s.

Mary Kay loved to look through all the dresses and pick the one she liked the best. The only problem she had was convincing the sales people that she really was allowed to buy her own clothing. "Where's your mother, little girl?" they would ask. Even when she put the money on the counter, the clerks sometimes made her call her mother at the restaurant for permission to buy something.

After spending about sixty cents on a dress, little Mary Kay would go to Kress, a

Because her mother was always working, Mary Kay learned early how to take care of herself in the big city of Houston, Texas.

five-and-dime store to buy herself lunch. She always had a pimento-cheese sandwich on toast with a soda, which cost twenty cents. Afterward, she would go to the movies. This was the favorite part of her day. For ten cents, she would see a whole afternoon of movies. Then the little girl would find her way back to the streetcar and home.

"Even though some of my duties were supposed to be too difficult for a child," she later said, "nobody ever told me that. As a result, I just *did* them." Years later, Mary Kay realized that her mother must have been very nervous about letting her child do so much on her own. She was careful to hide her worry, however. She gave her daughter the confidence she needed, and Mary Kay grew up with a lot of courage and belief in herself.

Aim for the Top!

Mary Kay's mother made her daughter feel good about herself. She also taught her daughter to compete with others as well as with herself. Since her mother was proud of her, Mary Kay aimed high.

Not only did Mary Kay want to get the best grades in the class, but she also wanted to be the best in everything. She tried to sell the most boxes of Girl Scout cookies and the most tickets to school dances. When she was in junior high, she learned how much fun it was to compete in school debates and other contests. Mary Kay also enjoyed typing and decided to become the best typist in the class. More than anything else, she wanted her own typewriter.

Mary Kay realized that her mother couldn't afford anything as expensive as a typewriter. Then one day Mrs. Wagner walked in with a large package. It was a typewriter. "To this day," Mary Kay says, "I don't know how long it took her to pay for

With her mother's support, Mary Kay learned the value of competition and building self-esteem. When she got a typewriter as a gift from her mother, Mary worked extra hard to be the best typist in her class.

that typewriter, or how she managed to get together the money for a down payment." Imagine how good Mary Kay felt when she brought home an award for the best typist in the class!

But Mrs. Wagner knew that you can't be the best all the time, so she also helped Mary Kay learn how to lose. She taught her daughter to look ahead when things got tough. "You can't win them all, Mary Kay," she said. "Tomorrow is another day." To this day, Mary Kay knows this is true. She knows people do learn from their failures. She says, "We fail forward to success."

Close Friends

Mary Kay also learned a great deal from her close friends Dorothy Zapp and Tillie Bass. Dorothy's family had more money than Mary Kay's family. Every day, Dorothy wore fancy dresses that her mother spent hours ironing. Her golden hair was curled into beautiful ringlets, too. Mary Kay walked over to Dorothy's house every day so they could go to school together. She waited patiently while Dorothy's mother tried to get her fragile child to eat her breakfast. When Mrs. Zapp wasn't looking, Dorothy would sneak her milk and jellied toast over to Mary Kay.

Since Mary Kay earned all A's, Mrs. Zapp wanted her to be Dorothy's friend. Mary Kay was happy to have a close friend and to get to eat such good food. She also enjoyed going with the Zapp family on their vacations and being at their holiday celebrations. Their Christmas tree was beautiful, strung with real popcorn and cranberries. Mary Kay didn't realize it at the time, but being friends with Dorothy made her compete even more. If Dorothy got an A, Mary Kay had to get an A+. Dorothy moved away when the girls graduated from high school, but they are friends to this day.

Mary Kay's friendship with Tillie Bass was also important. Like Dorothy, Tillie came from a family with more money than Mary Kay's. Her father was the chief of detectives in Houston. This impressed Mary Kay a great deal. Mrs. Bass treated Mary Kay like her own daughter. She worried about her emotional life and helped teach the child to cook and clean. Mary Kay worked hard to keep up with Tillie, who was eight years older. This friendship lasted a long time, too. Years later, when Mary Kay had to go to work to support her family, Tillie took care of Mary Kay's three small children. When Mary Kay became very rich in the 1980s, she invited Tillie and her husband to come to live in her big house in Dallas, Texas.

Learning About Sales

*Mary Kay's
enthusiasm
was catching.*
Mary Kay was sad when her
friends Dorothy and Tillie went to college.
She missed them, but she also felt jealous.
"It was my first experience of envy," she
said. What could she do to really top them?
Get married!

She was only 17 when she married Ben
Rogers in 1936. He would make a great
husband, she thought. A local radio star,
Ben sang in the evening with a group called
the Hawaiian Strummers. During the day,
he pumped gas at a filling station to earn
extra money. "I thought he was a tremen-
dous catch," she said, "sort of Houston's
Elvis Presley of that time." Even if she

couldn't afford to go to college, she had done better than her girlfriends, she thought.

Mary Kay soon realized that her desire to compete had led her down the wrong path. Her marriage was not happy. Since the couple had very little money, they lived in a bedroom in her mother's house in Houston. When Ben got a job in Dallas, they moved into their own house. Soon after, they had three children: Marylyn, Ben, and Richard. Mary Kay was barely out of her teen years.

Direct Sales

With three children, the budget was tight. Mary Kay needed a way to make some money that would still give her time to take care of her children. Ben was working in the filling station all day and playing in the band at night. Mary Kay turned to direct sales. In this type of selling, a salesperson does not work at a store. There are several ways to make a direct sale. The salesperson can go from door to door, telling people about the product. This is no longer very popular because most men and women work during the day. Also, most people will not open their door to a stranger.

Today, many direct salespeople call friends and acquaintances and ask them to set up "parties." Here's how it works. One customer hosts the party in his or her home. This customer then invites friends, neighbors, co-workers, and relatives to the party and serves food. The salesperson shows the products. If the party goes well, the guests will buy the products right then and there. Some guests will also want to host parties themselves. A few of the largest companies that use this sales method today are Avon, which sells cosmetics; Tupperware, which sells plastic goods; Amway, which sells cleaning supplies; and Mary Kay's company, Mary Kay Cosmetics.

Selling Books Door-to-Door

Mary Kay got the idea for direct sales from Ida Blake, a door-to-door saleswoman. Ida came to Mary Kay's house to try to sell her the *Child Psychology Bookshelf*. This set of books gave little lessons to teach children right from wrong. "I just thought those were the best books I'd ever seen!" Mary Kay said. But she did not have enough money to buy them.

Ida could see how much Mary Kay liked the books, so she let her keep them over the

One of Mary Kay's earliest sales jobs was selling books door-to-door in Texas.

weekend. Mary Kay read every page, and her enthusiasm grew. When Ida came to pick up the books, Mary Kay told her that she was going to save her money until she could afford a set. Ida said, "I'll tell you what, Mary Kay, if you sell ten sets of books for me, I'll give you a set."

Mary Kay sold all ten sets in a day and a half. She was so excited that everyone else got excited, too. Mary Kay's enthusiasm was catching. Ida couldn't believe it. "How did you *do* it?" she asked. Mary Kay had no idea that the books were hard to sell. Ida gave Mary Kay her free set of books—and a

job offer. Mary Kay accepted. In nine
months, she sold $25,000 worth of books.
She got to keep almost 40 percent of the
money—up to $10,000. Despite her success,
however, Mary Kay quit the job.

The people who bought the books were
unhappy. They blamed Mary Kay for making them buy the set. Her enthusiasm had
fired them up, too, but then they didn't use
the books. She knew that this wasn't her
fault. She still liked the books and thought
they were good. This experience taught her
that it's not enough that people buy a product. They also have to learn how to use it.

Giving Cookware Parties

Right after she quit, Ben lost his job at the
filling station. He was not making enough
in the band to support the family. What
could they do to earn a living? Mary Kay
and Ben decided to build on her experience
in direct sales. Working as a team, they
arranged house parties to sell special types
of cookware. These cook sets included pres-
sure cookers and double frying pans. The
hostess would gather several married
couples in her home. To sell the cookware,
Mary Kay and Ben showed how it worked
by cooking a meal in the hostess's home.

The meal was always the same—ham, green beans, sweet potatoes, and cake. Mary Kay bought the food during the day, and she and Ben carried everything to the home. The men sat in the living room with Ben as he explained all about the cookware and tried to make the sales. Mary Kay stayed in the kitchen, cooking the dinner. All the wives came into the kitchen and asked her, "Is it really as easy as it looks?" Mary Kay showed them how the cookware

To support themselves, Mary Kay and Ben arranged special house parties in order to sell cookware to other young couples.

worked. Even though Ben signed all the contracts, Mary Kay really made the sales. It was her hard work that paid off.

Mary Kay and Ben would usually eat what was left over after the selling party. If nothing was left, they went without dinner.

Methods That Sell Products

Mary Kay did not like to push people into buying things. This method, as she learned, is called the "hard sell." The hard sell made Mary Kay feel uncomfortable. She liked the "soft sell" better. This is a gentler form of persuasion. She wanted to teach people about a product and show how much she liked it. This way, she felt that a product would sell itself.

It was the 1930s, and the country was in the grip of the Great Depression. Many people were out of work. They did not have the money for a new set of pots and pans. Mary Kay learned that it is not enough that a product is good. People must have enough money to buy the product. It must also be something that people will buy even when they don't have a lot of money. Mary Kay knew that even in bad times people spend money for certain things, like going to the movies and buying makeup.

On Her Own

Selling sparked Mary Kay's urge to compete.

At the end of the 1930s, Ben was called to serve in World War II. When he returned in 1942, he told Mary Kay that he wanted a divorce. He had fallen in love with another woman. It was the lowest point in Mary Kay's life.

She felt that she had failed. Divorce was not common in the 1940s. She was so upset that she began to have medical problems. All her bones ached, and she had trouble walking. The doctors at a famous hospital told her that soon she would be disabled.

It's a "Man's World"

Mary Kay now found herself in her mother's position—only worse. Instead of having one small child to support, she had three. If that wasn't bad enough, she was also very ill. She felt terrible, but she did not have the time to feel sorry for herself.

Today, women compete with men in many different fields. But in the 1940s, things were different. It was a "man's world." Men were paid more than women for doing the same job. Men were also promoted more, even if women were doing a better job. Many women had worked while America's men were off fighting the war. Women had even held such traditional men's jobs as making airplanes, cars, and bridges. But when the war ended, women quit their jobs. Many women did not want to leave the work force, but they thought that the men should get their jobs back. When Mary Kay was divorced, it was very hard for a woman to get a job because all the men were coming back from the war.

Stanley Home Products

Mary Kay had been working at Stanley Home Products since Ben entered the army. She would call a friend and offer to show the products in that person's home, just as she had done with the cookware. This time, too, she did not make much money. She had to give three home parties a day to make enough money to support her family. She knew that if she looked sad people would not want to buy any of the products. She had to leave all her problems at home and look cheerful for her customers. Then a funny thing happened. The more Mary Kay acted happy, the happier she became. Finally, all her medical problems disappeared. Later, she decided that her sadness had caused her problems. Mary Kay had discovered that putting on a happy face made her feel happy.

But her life was still very hard. She was so busy that she had time for only three things: family, work, and church. She got up at five o'clock every morning to clean the house while her children slept. Then she fed her children breakfast and got them off to school. During the day, she gave two sales parties and rushed home to greet her children when they came home from school. She helped them with their homework, fixed their dinner, and tucked them into bed. When the babysitter arrived, Mary Kay was off to give another sales party. Everything seemed under control, but she didn't know what her son Richard was doing. When all was quiet at night, he would climb out of his bedroom window and sit on the curb to wait for his mother.

"Where's your mother?" the neighbors would ask.

"She's at a party," he always answered. He left out the part about the "party" being his mother's work.

The Urge to Compete

Selling sparked Mary Kay's urge to compete. The Stanley Home Product Company, like many direct-sales companies, used contests to get people to sell more. One time, the company announced that the salesperson who signed up the most new salespeople in one week would be crowned Miss Dallas. That's all Mary Kay had to hear. She sat right down and called everyone she knew. She would say:

"Hi, listen, Betty Ann, my company is planning to put some more people in your area, and I got to thinking, 'Whom do I know who would be just great doing what I do?' Well, naturally I thought of you."

Mary Kay wanted to win so much. And she did. She still has the ribbon. It made her think how important it is for people to be praised for their hard work.

Soon after, she got involved in another company contest—without even planning it. Stanley Home Products was holding its annual convention in Dallas, and Mary Kay decided to go. This, she thought, would be a good way to learn more about the company and about selling. She had to borrow $12 to pay for the train and hotel, and since she owned only two dresses, packing was

Mary Kay's competitive nature was sparked by a company sales contest in the 1940s. After taking notes at an annual convention, Mary Kay was sure she knew how to become the company's top seller.

26 ★ MADE IN AMERICA

easy. She wasn't sure if the $12 would cover food at the convention, so she brought along cheese and crackers.

She watched from the back row as the top saleswoman, the "Queen of Sales," was crowned. The queen's award was a beautiful alligator-skin handbag, which was very stylish in the 1940s. Mary Kay had wanted to be the queen so badly. Next year, she vowed, "I will be queen!" She begged the queen to put on a sales party so she could learn her selling methods. Mary Kay took 19 pages of notes and learned them by heart. She even marched right up to the president of the company and announced, "Next year I am going to be the queen!" The president didn't laugh at her. He looked her right in the eye and said, "You know, somehow I think you will." At the time, Mary Kay was making seven dollars a week in sales. She was probably the lowest-paid person in the company.

No one was surprised when, at the end of the year, Mary Kay was crowned Queen of Sales. But she was disappointed. The prize had been changed. She didn't get the alligator bag. From this, Mary Kay learned that prizes have to be things that people really want.

A year after she attended the annual convention and decided to become her company's top seller, Mary Kay was crowned Queen of Sales.

Saving Time Around the House

Mary Kay wanted to spend more time with her children and less time cooking and cleaning. Her children helped a lot with household tasks—like raking leaves, taking out the trash, and doing the laundry—but she still felt too rushed. She decided to hire a full-time housekeeper. "Why not write a dream ad?" she thought. "I need a person to cook, clean, care for my three children, and so on," she wrote. "Anybody's who's crazy enough to answer this ad is really asking for it," she thought.

A wonderful woman answered the ad, and Mary Kay hired her on the spot. She was thrilled that the woman accepted the job. Then Mary Kay stopped and thought about what she had done. She didn't have enough money to pay her. That Monday, Mary Kay went to work being even more motivated than usual. Because her housekeeper had to be paid, Mary Kay decided to increase her goal for sales from that day forward. She made her goal, and much more. The housekeeper stayed with the family for nine years.

Mary Kay learned other ways to make more time for important things, like her family and church. Since she had hired the housekeeper, Mary Kay had started sleeping until six o'clock in the morning. She no longer had to get up at five o'clock to do the housework. "Why not keep getting up at five o'clock?" she thought. If she got an extra hour a day, in a week she would have a whole extra day. So Mary Kay started what she calls the "Five O'Clock Club." Even today, she still gets up at five in the morning to read reports, finish paperwork, and organize her day.

4

Beauty by Mary Kay

*"Much of the time
I was...held back by
outdated ideas of what
a woman should and
should not do when
working with men."*
Mary Kay worked in direct
sales for 25 years. For 13 years, she sold
cleaning supplies for Stanley Home Products. When she remarried and moved to St.
Louis, Missouri, she sold home furnishings
for World Gift. One day she decided to quit.

Unfair Treatment

One reason Mary Kay left her job at World
Gift was her anger at the way she was being
treated because she was a woman. Most of
the men in the company did not take
women seriously. She was furious every
time she had a great idea and the men in

the room said "Mary Kay, you're thinking just like a woman." She was also passed over for promotions. "Nothing would make me angrier than training some man only to have him become my superior," she said. For six months she would train a man to sell. Then when they returned to Dallas, he would get promoted—only because he was a man. There was also the matter of money.

Mary Kay and the other women at the company were doing the same work as the men, but they were making only half the money. It seemed to her that a woman's brains were worth only fifty cents on the dollar in a male-run company. "Men have families to support," she was told. She knew that women had families to support, too. After all, she was one of those women. Years later, Mary Kay said, "Much of the time I was actually handicapped or held back by outdated ideas of what a woman should and should not do when working with men."

Making a Wish List

After she left World Gift, Mary Kay decided to write a book about her experiences in direct sales. She hoped that she could offer advice and help other people become good

After leaving her position at World Gift, Mary Kay decided to write a book about her experiences as a woman in business.

salespeople, too. She knew the book would help women who wanted to work. Writing would also help her get rid of some of the bitterness she felt at the unfair treatment she had gotten as a woman in business.

She began her book with two lists. On one side she wrote all the good things about her experiences. On the other side, she wrote all the bad things. Looking at the good things, Mary Kay thought, "This looks like a dream company. If I started my dream company, what else would I need?"

First off, Mary Kay would give women the best possible chance to earn a lot of money. How could she pay the best commission, the percentage of money from each sale? She knew that dealing in cash would save everyone money. If there are no bad debts to collect, the loss won't be passed on to the salespeople or the customers. Next, she would make sure that women had an equal chance to get ahead. "I structured my company so that everything was black and white. You knew exactly what you had to do to succeed," she said later. She would also get rid of assigned territories—she would let her salespeople take their sales forces anywhere they wanted.

Mary Kay also wanted to change the way people think about business. Her ideal company would focus on giving, not getting. It would be based on the Golden Rule: Do unto others as you would have them do unto you. No hard sell, either. Mary Kay wanted to teach as much as sell. She didn't want customers to have to wait a long time for their products to arrive. She decided to make sure that she sold only a few things so every salesperson could have a big stock on hand. Finally, all her products would come with a money-back guarantee.

Finding the Ideal Product

The longer Mary Kay thought about her dream company, the more she liked it. "I'd love to work for an organization like this," she thought. Being Mary Kay, she wasn't happy only dreaming about something. She was going to make it happen. First, she needed a product to sell.

One day, Mary Kay was holding a Stanley Home party when she noticed something odd about all the women in the room. Every one had beautiful skin. It couldn't be their ages, Mary Kay thought, because there were women of all ages in the group. It didn't seem to be the lights either. What could have given all these women such nice skin?

At the end of the party, the hostess handed all her guests a set of little bottles. It took Mary Kay a few days to work up the courage to try the creams in these bottles. That afternoon, her son came home and kissed her on the cheek. "Gee, Mom, you feel smooth!" he said. Mary Kay was very curious. What had she put on her face?

The woman who had hosted the party explained that her father had made the creams. He had been a tanner, a person who uses chemicals to soften leather. He noticed that his hands stayed soft and smooth, while the rest of his skin aged. He began to try some of the mixture on his face. It got as smooth as his hands. There was just one catch: The stuff smelled so bad that no one wanted to use it. Only his daughter stood behind him. She took the formulas and created gentle, nice-smelling lotions and creams.

Mary Kay decided to buy the formulas. She took them to a cosmetics factory and had them made up and packaged. They were called Night Cream, Cleansing Cream, Skin Freshener, and Day Radiance. She added a few luxury products like lipsticks. In all, she had ten different products. She thought this was a good selection but not too much for the salespeople in her dream company to keep in stock.

A Company Is Born—Or Is It?

Mary Kay had a plan and products, but there was so much more to do to start a company. What about the legal and financial details? Mary Kay's second husband had many years of experience running a vitamin company. She turned over control of this side of the business to him. This left Mary Kay free to hire and train people.

Against great odds, Mary Kay started her own cosmetics company in 1963. Her ability to take charge and inspire others made her destined for success.

Mary Kay wanted to get the best possible salespeople, so she called many of her longtime friends. Most of them were eager to work in her new company. She also had to set up an office. She set up right in the middle of many other office buildings. She spent all the money she had—$5,000—for the skin-cream formulas, jars, and used office equipment. She decided to name her new company Beauty by Mary Kay.

Tragedy Strikes

It was exactly a month before Beauty by Mary Kay was set to open. Mary Kay and her husband were having breakfast and talking about their plans. Suddenly, he had a heart attack and died.

Mary Kay had to make a decision. Should she forget about her plans or go ahead? She had been counting on her husband to run the legal and business parts of the company. Mary Kay knew she wouldn't be able to run her company alone. She turned to people whom she trusted for advice.

"Mary Kay," her lawyer said, "there is no way your company will succeed. Sell everything now and get back whatever cash you can. If you don't, you'll end up penniless."

Mary Kay Cosmetics

"If she [Mary Kay] can do it, so can I."

Mary Kay decided to turn to her family for advice. On the day of her husband's funeral, her two sons and her daughter gathered in Dallas. After the services, they sat in Mary Kay's living room. They listened in silence while she told them what her lawyer had said.

Plunging In

"I've decided I want to go ahead with the company," she told them. "Will you help me?" Richard, her youngest child, was just 20 years old. He was doing very well selling life insurance. "Will you come help me guide my new company?" she asked him. "I can't give you very much money, but I need you." He accepted at once.

Ben was 27 years old. He had a wife and two small children and was working as a welder. "I can't join you right now," he said. Then he reached into his pocket and took out his bankbook. Calmly, he handed it to his mother. It had $4,500, all the money he had saved since high school. "Mother," he said, "I think you could do anything in the world that you wanted to. Here's my savings. If this will help you in any way, I want you to have it." About a year later, Ben quit his job and joined the company to run the warehouse. About the same time, Mary Kay's daughter, Marylyn, became the very first Mary Kay director in Houston.

Mary Kay's children had shouted, "You can do it!" That's all Mary Kay needed. She was off!

Getting Started

It's clear that Mary Kay is not superstitious. The company opened its doors in November 1963, on the traditional bad-luck day, Friday the 13th. Could she succeed when all the experts had said that she would fail? What would she have to do to succeed?

First off, since Richard was so young, Mary Kay asked him to wear a suit and tie. Not only would he look older, but the company would also seem more professional. But his suit created a problem. The store was too small to have much storage space. The stock was about two blocks away. After a customer bought something, Richard would have to hurry over to the warehouse, run down a flight of stairs, and bring the item up from the basement. He couldn't do this in a suit and tie. So he'd pull off his jacket and tie, grab the item, race back to the store, and slip his jacket and tie back on. Mary Kay could see that something had to be done. That's when she hired her other son, Ben, to run the warehouse.

Mary Kay, Richard, and Ben worked 16 to 18 hours every day to build the business. After the store closed, they would pack orders, write newsletters, and pay bills. All their hard work paid off. It can take many years for a company to make money, but Mary Kay made a profit after only the first three months. The company sold $198,000 the first year. The second year, the total sales increased more than four times—to $800,000. Business was so good that within a year Mary Kay's company was able to move to larger, more convenient offices. The company now had three offices, a room in which to train salespeople, and a huge warehouse. Mary Kay said that the new building felt like the Grand Canyon after their cramped space. She also changed the company's name to Mary Kay Cosmetics, Inc.

Building a Major Corporation

Less than a year later, on September 13, 1964, Mary Kay gathered all her employees in a big meeting that she called a seminar. Two hundred people sat in the warehouse to celebrate their success. The budget was still tight, so Mary Kay cooked all the food herself. She strung crepe paper and balloons across the ceiling and hired a band. Mary Kay never forgot what the alligator bag had meant to her. To thank the people who had worked very hard for her, she gave them awards. In the early days, these prizes were small, because the company was still struggling.

Mary Kay still holds these seminars and award ceremonies. Now, more than 100,000 people attend. Today, the awards are a lot bigger: mink coats, pink Cadillacs, precious gems, and fabulous vacations.

Mary Kay had always liked sales contests with great prizes. For her company, prizes started small but would eventually be expensive clothes and big pink Cadillac cars.

Mary Kay's pink Cadillacs are so famous that General Motors calls the color "Mary Kay pink." The Queen of Sales for Mary Kay's company is presented with a satin sash, a bouquet of roses, a diamond tiara, a mink coat, and a diamond ring.

By 1968, the company had grown so much that Mary Kay decided to build her own factory to make the cosmetics. Today, the manufacturing plant is bigger than three football fields. Nearly 50,000 jars of

Today, Mary Kay's annual conventions are like giant parties that celebrate the company's success. Here, Mary Kay leaves the convention stage with some of her top salespeople.

facial cream are made a day. The original 10 products have grown to over 150 items. More than 500 people work in the manufacturing part of the company.

In 1968, Mary Kay Cosmetics became a public company and offered stock for sale. The stock sold so well that Mary Kay became a millionaire. The poor little girl from the wrong side of the tracks had finally made it. But she didn't think, "Wow, I'm a millionaire. *Now* I'm happy!" The real thrill was being able to do what she loved. That's why Mary Kay still gets up at five o'clock every morning to do her work.

Another Personal Tragedy

In 1966, Mary Kay married Mel Ash, a salesman. They were very happy together, and Mel helped Mary Kay with the business. In 1980, the doctors told Mel that he was dying of cancer. Mary Kay decided to stay home and nurse him. For seven weeks, she did not go to the office. Mel died on Monday, July 7, 1980. The next day, the entire company would be going to St. Louis, Missouri, for a big meeting called a jamboree. More than 7,500 people would be attending. Mary Kay went to the funeral on Tuesday, and tried to put aside her grief to attend the jamboree on Friday. She tried to show the happiness she felt for all her employees, rather than her own sadness.

Promises Made Good

In 1985, Mary Kay and Richard bought back the company's stock. The deal was worth more than $460 million. (The company had made a profit of $323 million in

1983.) By 1989, the company's profits had risen to more than $400 million. Today, they are still rising.

Mary Kay had kept her promises to herself. Her company was a place that gave women a shot at the top. "We still have more women who make more than fifty thousand dollars per year than any other company," she said in a recent interview. Today, there are nearly 200,000 women on the Mary Kay sales force. "The struggles they face are all problems I've experienced," Mary Kay notes. "I know what it's like to be a single mother supporting a family." The people who work for Mary Kay look at her and think, "If she can do it, so can I." People around the country know that Mary Kay is a strong supporter of women's rights.

Mary Kay has received many awards for her achievements. In 1978, she was given the Horatio Alger Award. Three years later, the American Academy of Achievements gave her the Gold Plate Award. She has also received the Cosmetic Career Woman of the Year and the Direct Selling Hall of Fame awards. *Business Week* magazine named her one of America's top businesswomen. In 1979, she was featured on television's "60 Minutes," which did a profile of her

Happy Cadillac winners celebrate their success at a Mary Kay convention in Dallas, Texas.

and her company. And in 1984, a book called *The 100 Best Companies to Work for in America* listed Mary Kay Cosmetics.

Mary Kay also serves on many charities. She volunteers her time for the American Cancer Society. In 1990, she served as the honorary chairperson of the Texas Crusade for the American Cancer Society.

"You can do it, Mary Kay!" her mother had always said. And, for sure, her mother was right!

Glossary

assigned territories Areas salespeople are given to work in, with no possibility of selling elsewhere.

commission A percentage of money from a sale that is given to a salesperson.

direct sales A type of selling in which a salesperson calls on a customer directly. Direct sales do not take place in stores.

sanatorium A special hospital for people who are suffering from certain diseases, such as tuberculosis.

seminar In business, a big meeting at which company members learn ways to do their jobs better.

stock Ownership in a company that the public acquires by buying shares in it.

For Further Reading

Ash, Mary Kay. *Mary Kay*. New York: Harper and Row, 1981.

Barrett, Linda, and Guengerich, Galen. *Sales and Distribution*. New York: Franklin Watts, 1991.

Dunnan, Nancy. *Entrepreneurship*. Englewood Cliffs, NJ: Silver Burdett Press, 1990.

Stefoff, Rebecca. *Mary Kay Ash: Mary Kay, a Beautiful Business*. Ada, OK: Barrett Educational Corporation, 1992.

Index

Photo Credits:

Cover: ©John F. Rhodes/Dallas Morning News; p. 4: Dallas Morning News; p. 35: ©Clint Grant/Dallas Morning News; p. 42: ©Clint Grant/Dallas Morning News; p. 45: ©Ken Geiger/Dallas Morning News.

Illustrations by Ron Jones.